a year in the life of **the welsh marches** derry brabbs

FRANCES LINCOLN

a year in the life of the welsh marches derry brabbs

Frances Lincoln Limited
4 Torriano Mews
Torriano Avenue
London NW5 2RZ
www.franceslincoln.com

A YEAR IN THE LIFE OF THE WELSH MARCHES
Copyright © 2007 Frances Lincoln Limited

Text and photographs copyright © 2007 Derry Brabbs
Map on page 6 by Martin Bagness
Edited and designed by Jane Havell Associates

First Frances Lincoln edition 2007

Many thanks to
The Ludlow Festival
English Heritage
The Landmark Trust

TITLE PAGE: Stokesay Castle in winter

British Library cataloguing-in-publication data
A catalogue record for this book is available from the British Library

ISBN 978 0 7112 2635 7

Printed in Singapore

9 8 7 6 5 4 3 2 1

contents

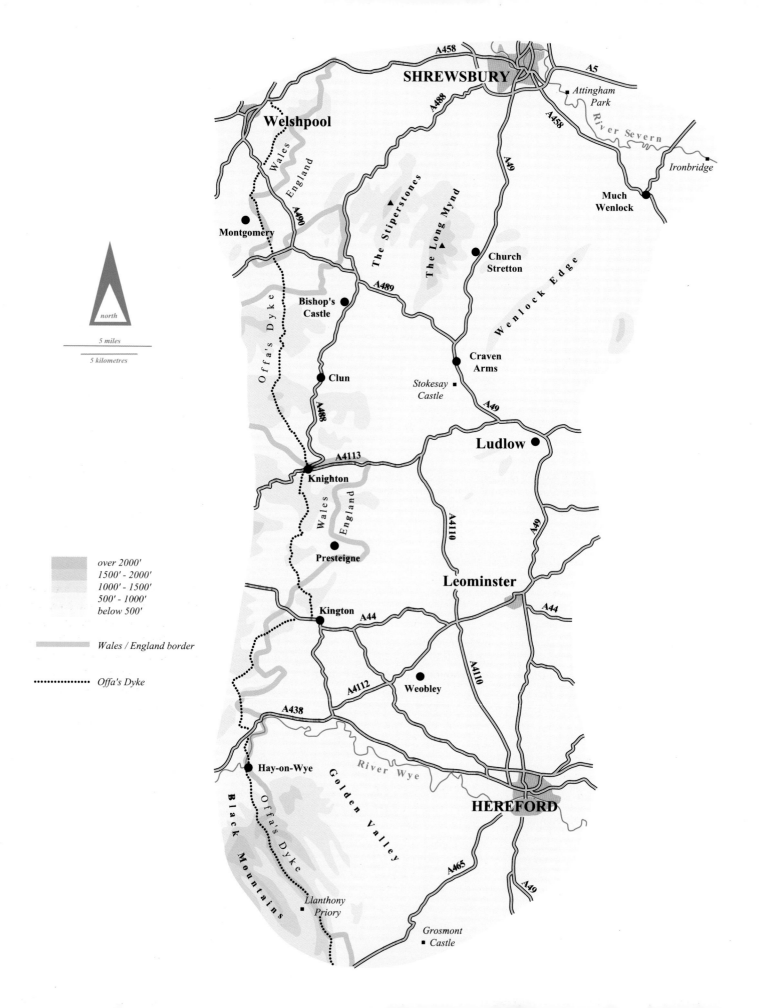

the welsh marches
introduction

RIGHT: With the exception of the Wye towards the south, the border-delineating rivers of the Marches are not the wide, sweeping bodies of water associated with international boundaries. Presteigne, Radnorshire, sits on the south bank of the Lugg in Powys; just a few yards across the old packhorse bridge lies the English county of Herefordshire. Presteigne's former importance can be readily gauged by its number of rather grand-looking Georgian buildings; although many are now private houses, there were also up to thirty inns to cater for a diverse clientele ranging from cattle-drovers to lawyers attending the Quarter Sessions once held there.

OVERLEAF: At the heart of the Shropshire Hills, the Cardingmill Valley is typical of the deep, narrow incisions that cut into the bulk of the Long Mynd. Narrow paths follow streams up towards their source, before breaking out on to the open moor, covered with networks of ancient tracks and the tell-tale humps and bumps of tumuli and hill forts.

The Welsh Marches are defined as the border areas dividing England and Wales. The word 'march' has evolved linguistically from *marca*, Latin for border, and similar derivations with identical meanings can be found in other modern European languages. In strictly geographic terms, the Marches could be deemed to extend from the Dee estuary in the north to the River Severn in the south of Wales. However, the accepted interpretation has always been that the Welsh Marches comprise the western fringes of Shropshire and Herefordshire, and the eastern part of the corresponding counties across the border in Wales.

Although perhaps no longer the closely guarded secret they used to be, the Marches contain some of England's most beautiful and unspoilt countryside. It seems quite extraordinary that the Industrial Revolution was acknowledged to have started little more than a dozen miles away, by the River Severn at Ironbridge. In recognition of the Marches' importance in terms of landscape, flora and fauna, large segments of the region have been afforded varying degrees of environmental protection. The Shropshire Hills were among the first areas in England to be officially designated an Area of Outstanding Natural Beauty (AONB), back in 1958.

Within the boundaries of the AONB, more specific segments, such as important wildlife habitats, are further protected by their Environmentally Sensitive Area (ESA) status; many other smaller areas are Sites of Special Scientific Interest (SSSIs). There are always voices raised against such restrictions on development and use, often on the basis of hearsay rather than fact, but the reality is that the countryside we tend to take for granted is a fragile and finite resource. The majority of landowners and visitors certainly respect the countryside in which they work and play, but the small percentage who do not have a disproportionate capacity to wreak irrevocable damage that might take generations to repair.

The irregular landscape of the Shropshire hills and valleys contains many hill forts, earthworks and Norman castles. The region endured centuries of turbulence as a disputed border territory; long before the arrival of the Romans, the Celtic Cornovii tribe had established a network of forts whose outlines are still prominent on almost every hilltop. It was from those bastions that Caractacus and the Welsh tribes battled against the advancing Roman legions.

One of the most dramatic natural features of the Marches is the Long Mynd (from the Welsh *myndd*, meaning mountain). Located roughly midway between Shrewsbury and Ludlow, it consists of a range of hills some 9.5km/ 6 miles in length which in places rises to a height of around 518m/1,700 feet. The whole range is penetrated by deep-cut valleys, referred to locally as 'batches', which would have provided perfect terrain from which to wage guerrilla warfare against enemies unfamiliar with the landscape.

Although perhaps not quite matching up to the natural splendours of the Long Mynd, Wenlock Edge or surrounding hills, Offa's Dyke certainly stamps its own visual authority upon the landscape. Named after the Anglo-Saxon King Offa, who ruled Mercia from 757 to 796 AD, the earthwork and ditch created a defensible border that survives as an awesome

reminder of the sense of fear once generated by the Welsh. At the height of his powers, Offa's jurisdiction spread far beyond central England to include East Anglia and Kent, and he was also able to forge alliances with Wessex and Northumbria through the marriage of his daughters into their ruling families.

William I (1066–87) also discovered that his plans for a universally subjugated nation might take just a bit longer to execute than envisaged; the Celtic tribes were as unenthusiastic about being ruled by Normans as they had been when the Romans attempted it several centuries earlier. The Marches became an uneasy frontier zone in which the English king was obliged to create the earldoms of Chester, Shrewsbury and Hereford. He entrusted those jurisdictions to his close relatives and most trusted aides in the hope that they might stamp his authority by proxy upon the troublesome area.

This collection of Marcher lordships given out to barons, knights and bishops effectively became mini-states, ruled from the safety of well-fortified strongholds. Unlike their counterparts in other parts of England, the Marcher lords were not directly accountable to the king and were able to establish and administer their own laws, exact taxes for their own benefit and build castles without recourse to the customary royal grant. However, despite all their efforts and for a considerable period after the Conquest, Norman territorial acquisitions were largely restricted to the lowland areas either side of Offa's Dyke.

By around 1300, the Marches had become more stable and their distinctive society embraced both native and immigrant languages – Welsh, English and French. The new rulers were able to devote more time to establishing stone castles to house themselves in greater style and comfort; they built new churches and brought monks over from France to establish abbeys and priories which were endowed with generous gifts of land. Many of those medieval structures survive to the present day, albeit as atmospheric ruins in the case of the

castles and monastic institutions. However, many of the churches built by the Normans and their successors remain intact; either in the form in which they were originally created, or enlarged and extended but with the original architecture remaining as a dominant feature.

The larger towns and cities within the border region, such as Shrewsbury and Hereford, were already established as important centres in their own right prior to the Conquest; Ludlow, however, owes its existence to the Norman occupation. It is the most impressive of all the border fortresses and, in medieval times, a thriving market town evolved from the planned development that spread eastwards from the castle walls. Timber-framed buildings and old coaching inns remain important features of this prosperous town, which was once set on an important coaching network. With elegant Georgian brick architecture acting as a perfect foil to the black-and-white core of the town, Ludlow remains one of the most satisfying and enjoyable places to explore in Britain.

Literary associations with the Marches are legion. The poetry of A. E. Housman (1859–1936) is frequently quoted in guidebooks to describe physical characteristics of the land. Though his epic work, *A Shropshire Lad*, is dark in mood and focuses more on human mortality than on extolling the virtues of the Shropshire countryside, the 63 separate poems do contain references to specific places. Mary Webb (1881–1927) and Bruce Chatwin (1940–89) wrote novels set in the remote valleys and hill farms of the Welsh Borders. *Gone to Earth* and *On the Black Hill* convey a strong sense of how living and working in such an environment affected both family relationships and individual outlooks on life. In terms of non-fiction documentary writing, the Kilvert diaries are considered by some to be minor classics and of significant social historical value. Francis Kilvert was a Victorian country parson who, from 1870 to 1879, kept a journal about his own activities and day-

ABOVE, FAR LEFT: The tiny church of St Giles at Pipe Aston, Herefordshire, is one of several architectural gems in the Marches. Although parts of the building's fabric were restored during the thirteenth and fourteenth centuries, the original Norman tympanum over the north doorway appears as perfectly preserved as the day it was created. The quality of the craftsmanship that carved this depiction of the Agnus Dei is outstanding and the tableau is perfectly encased within the zig-zag patterned arch.

ABOVE, LEFT: Herefordshire is richly endowed with perfectly preserved examples of the earliest post-Conquest Romanesque style of architecture, a blend of imported Norman and Celtic. For sheer artistry, St Mary and St David, Kilpeck, Herefordshire, is the most impressive. The pillars are adorned with a pair of snakes with tails in their mouths, symbolising the unending cycle of life and death.

ABOVE: Through its geographical location and architectural heritage, Ludlow in Shropshire represents the very essence of the Welsh Marches. The town's recorded history begins in 1086 when the castle was first established on a hill overlooking the rivers Teme and Corve, built as part of a network within the border region to subdue both the Welsh and enclaves of independently minded Saxons who thought little of their new rulers. A planned town was laid out around the castle and rapidly expanded when Ludlow was established as the main garrison and administrative centre of the Marches. Flourishing trade and industry brought prosperity. The town is renowned for its dramatic half-timbered Tudor buildings and elegant brick Georgian town houses and mansions.

to-day life in the parishes with which he was involved through his ministry.

The pastoral tranquillity that abounds in parts of Herefordshire has attracted many refugees from the cities, anxious to escape the pressures of urban living and to re-evaluate their lives. Some of these incomers have brought a desire to embrace fully all aspects of rural living, building award-winning eco-housing and promoting the spread of organic farming and fruit growing. Many farmers in the Marches have never been anything but organic, and they must welcome the increased demand from twenty-first-century consumers to know where their food comes from and whether chemicals have been used in its production.

The physical characteristics of the Marches very much dictate its agricultural practices: in the space of just a few miles, one can travel from broad swathes of cereal crops to high moorland pastures grazed by hardy breeds of sheep. The Hereford is one of Britain's best-known cattle breeds and has evolved from the indigenous red cattle that once roamed the area. The breed's first official Herd Book was started in 1846 and contained the records of over 500 bulls, entered by 75 breeders. The distinctive dark-coloured descendants of those original animals have been exported to more than 25 countries worldwide and their beef is unsurpassable in taste and texture.

Herefordshire has also long been associated with the cider and perry industries, with large tracts of land given over to fruit growing. As with the beer industry, there is a world of difference between a commercially manufactured, mass-market product and the independently brewed variety. It is extraordinary how utterly different the two can be both in taste and colour; on occasions, it is difficult to credit them with the same origins.

None of the cross-border roads between England and Wales has been expanded into a dual carriageway; life today in the Welsh Marches seems to be conducted at an agreeably moderate pace. Villages and smaller market towns give the impression that most people living and working there have stayed through choice. A refreshing sense of community prevails. Although it would be naive to suggest that the border counties do not suffer from the same pressures of modern life as more urban areas, to be surrounded by such gloriously rich countryside must have more than a transient effect on a person's wellbeing and outlook on life.

The Welsh Marches are a national treasure. One can only hope that such a precious environment receives the love and protection it deserves for the education and enjoyment of future generations.

offa's dyke

Offa's Dyke – a linear, ditch-and-bank earthwork that loosely follows the line of the England–Wales border – bears the name of the Anglo-Saxon king who instigated its construction during the latter decades of the eighth century. Just as Hadrian's Wall was built to prevent cross-border incursions by hostile Scottish and northern tribes, the dyke was intended to perform the same function and keep the native Welsh at bay. Standing on top of a surviving banked section, one can fully appreciate what a mammoth undertaking it was, a piece of civil engineering that would not be surpassed for another millennium with the excavation of England's canal network. Offa (757–96 AD) must have wielded a considerable degree of power over the civilian population in order to muster a labour force big enough to execute his plans. Even if individual communities were solely responsible for their own local sector, the amount of earth that had to be shifted, using rudimentary hand tools, must have been daunting.

Written evidence from Offa's reign is scarce, as that period of Anglo-Saxon history was only just emerging from the shadows of the Dark Ages ('dark' relating more to a dearth of information than to any barbaric practices meted out to the population!). The Welsh monk, Asser, mentioned Offa and the dyke in his ninth-century biography of Alfred the Great, stating that it ran 'from sea to sea', a statement that led some experts to deduce erroneously that all earthworks between the Dee estuary in the north and the River Wye in the south were attributable to Offa. However, the central sections over some of the most dramatic landscape of the Marches were indisputably the work of the Mercian king. At the height of his reign, Offa controlled most of England from south of the Humber, introduced the English silver penny to facilitate trade with Charlemagne's France and visited Rome to forge links with the papacy. Despite all those notable achievements, however, he will always be remembered most for his ditch.

OPPOSITE, BELOW: Despite its contours being diminished by the passage of time, the section of dyke running high above Knighton clearly displays what a formidable obstacle it must have originally presented to Welsh invaders. Displaced earth from its west-facing ditch was piled up into a bank on the Mercian side to create a barrier some 25 metres wide and up to 8 metres high from ditch to bank top. It appears to have been carefully aligned to present an open view into Wales from along its length.

BELOW: The dyke's ascent up towards the summit of Llanfair Hill is typical of many sections of the south Shropshire Hills. From a distance the scene appears one of verdant rural tranquillity, with farmsteads nestling in valley bottoms and the dyke's course clearly marked by broad-leaved trees of varying vintages that have made their home on the bank top. For walkers, the reality can be rather different: the inclines are deceptively steep in places and fighting one's way uphill over slippery mud and exposed, tangled roots can be remorselessly energy-sapping.

RIGHT: The nineteenth-century Offa's Stone marks the route of the dyke where it crosses the road linking Presteigne and Knighton. Its proclamation that Offa constructed the dyke in 757 AD might be somewhat over-enthusiastic, as that was the first year of his 39-year reign – even the most accomplished engineer with modern plant and machinery would be hard-pressed to complete such a task in twelve months.

LEFT: Much of the dyke is still traceable along the 130km/80 miles from the Wye Valley to Wrexham. In the more remote upland areas, it retains much of its original impressive stature while in other parts it has disappeared altogether due to years of agriculture. On farmland where the dyke either coincides with, or has itself formed, field boundaries, its course is reduced to little more than a gentle undulation.

BELOW: The Offa's Dyke Path was officially designated as a National Trail in 1971. During its 285-km/177-mile journey, it passes through eight different counties and crosses the border between England and Wales twenty times. The Trail also links three Areas of Outstanding Natural Beauty, one of which is the Shropshire Hills. This section of the dyke, perched high above the border town of Knighton, is arguably one of the most atmospheric on the entire route as it twines itself around the contours of the exposed, Welsh-facing slopes.

OPPOSITE: Sheep are now the sole guardians of Offa's Dyke, thriving on the vast tracts of rich grassland that extend up from the valleys to all but the highest ridges. Although perhaps no longer under threat from cross-border rustlers, they face new hazards in the form of litter or ill-managed dogs brought by increased numbers of walkers. Happily, most of those who walk the dyke are mindful of the basic common sense of the Country Code, but there always seem to be a minority who wilfully discard cans, bottles and assorted non-biodegradable picnic debris.

marcher castles

LEFT: New Radnor, Radnorshire, is still overshadowed by the giant motte of its Norman castle. Although the village was newly built rather than being a subjugated Saxon settlement, the setting perfectly illustrates what a terrifying, looming presence those structures must have presented to local inhabitants. Despite being later consolidated in stone, New Radnor Castle was destroyed and rebuilt several times during violent cross-border conflicts over three centuries. Its final engagement was during the Civil War in 1644, when it fell to Cromwell's forces after a brief siege. All that now remains of the castle's walls, towers and keep is a collection of assorted banks, ditches and grassy hummocks.

Although traces of Iron Age hill forts can still be found on the highest ground of the Welsh Marches, more tangible evidence of the region's turbulent past survives in the numerous castles that sprang up in the wake of the Norman Conquest. From simple earth mounds to monumental stone ruins, they stand as a stark reminder of that period in British history when ruthless invaders imposed their will upon a largely helpless population. An extract from one of the great historical documents of that early medieval period, *The Anglo-Saxon Chronicle*, leaves the reader in no doubt about how the Norman presence was viewed at that time: 'They filled the land full of castles. They cruelly oppressed the wretched men of the land with castle works and when the castles were made, they filled them with devils and evil men.'

The first fortifications used by the Normans to secure and dominate their newly seized territories were motte and bailey castles, relatively simple and speedy to execute with gangs of forced labour from the local population. The motte was an inverted pudding-basin-shaped mound of earth, topped by a defensive wooden palisade. These earth mounds were referred to in Shropshire as 'tumps' and across the border in Wales as 'tomen', a word with the additional, more derogatory, meaning of dung hill. The deep ditch created by the motte's excavation became an outer defensive ring that encompassed the main living area, the bailey. That space would have been large enough to accommodate living quarters and a section where livestock could be kept out of harm's way. Outward-facing

wooden spikes would be used to secure the ditch, which might be surrounded by further spiked palisades or turned into a moat through the diversion of nearby streams.

In the more settled decades that followed the initial post-Conquest turmoil and right through the twelfth century, the Marcher lords consolidated their holdings by building castles in stone. Relatively few mottes were converted to stone as the sites were too unstable to bear its weight safely; rebuilding took place on more strategic, naturally defended sites. Those castles that have survived the combined ravages of time and the elements vary from fragile, overgrown fragments of walls or crumbled towers to magnificent edifices such as Ludlow, the eventual power base and administrative centre of the Marches.

LEFT: Grosmont Castle, Monmouthshire, was founded around 1070 by William Fitz Osbern on a strategic site overlooking the River Monnow which forms the border with England. The substantial remains visible today are largely attributable to Hubert de Burgh (Regent to the infant Henry III) who remodelled it during the early thirteenth century. It had been the administrative centre for a sensitive border sector that included two other fortresses in the same ownership, Skenfrith and White Castle: together they formed a defensive triangle known as the Three Castles. After de Burgh's death, Grosmont reverted to royal ownership and in 1267 was granted to Henry III's second son, Prince Edmund, who adopted it as one of his main residences.

BELOW: Skenfrith is the lowest-lying of the Three Castles, using the River Monnow as a natural defence barrier against one wall. A tributary was dug to divert water round the rest of the site to augment the existing fortifications and feed a mill to the south – but, as Hubert de Burgh discovered to his cost during building works in 1219, water can easily turn from an ally into an enemy. Severe flooding wreaked havoc and devastated the castle. Rather than struggle on with repairs, de Burgh pragmatically filled the interior of the ruined site with river gravel and used that as the foundation for a new building.

LEFT: The stone castle high above the small market town of Montgomery was built during the reign of Henry III, replacing an earlier motte and bailey a mile away. The rocky north–south ridge provided far-reaching views and ample early warning of danger. However, the castle was still vulnerable from more level ground to the south-west and the inner ward was protected by ditches, drawbridges and towers. Peace reduced its strategic importance and by 1343, a century old, it was falling into disrepair. It was restored by Roger Mortimer, 2nd Earl of March, and two centuries later by Henry VIII. Like many other Marches castles, it succumbed to ruin after Parliamentarian siege during the Civil War.

ABOVE: Clun Castle, Shropshire, began its history as a motte and bailey, built by the Norman Robert de Say during the mid-twelfth century as part of the Marcher lordship the Barony of Clun. It was strategically sited on a rocky outcrop near the confluence of the Usk and Clun rivers, overlooking an ancient track used to drive livestock from Wales to markets in the Midlands. It later came into the ownership of the Fitzalan family, who built it into a formidable stone edifice. However, their principal holding was Arundel in Sussex (now home to the Dukes of Norfolk who still hold the Clun title); after they abandoned Clun in favour of England's south coast in 1270, the castle gradually fell into decline.

ABOVE AND LEFT: Stokesay Castle, one of the outstanding buildings of the Welsh Marches, is not actually a castle but a magnificently preserved thirteenth-century fortified manor house. The site originated as an austere Norman stronghold, but began its transformation when purchased by a wealthy local wool merchant, Laurence of Ludlow, in 1281. The most remarkable aspect of the building's appearance, both inside and out, is just how little it has been altered and its astonishing state of preservation some seven centuries after it was created. The castle has two towers joined by a buttressed Great Banqueting Hall with long, gothic, gabled windows. Massive roof timbers, made from whole trees, dominate the Great Hall. An original staircase leads up to Stokesay's most endearing feature (left), a timber-framed suite of living accommodation. This was erected on top of the building's oldest segment, the north tower of 1240, and looks for all the world like an elaborate set of medieval dormer windows.

LEFT: Acton Burnell Castle, Shropshire, is another example of a fortified manor house whose emphasis was more on residential comfort than the ability to withstand a serious assault. The owner, Robert Burnell, was Bishop of Bath and Wells, and also Chancellor to Edward I, who granted him a licence to crenellate the castle in 1284. It was constructed of red sandstone and consisted of a central two-storey building containing all the principal rooms. Continuity of ownership appears to be a key factor in whether such ancient buildings survive – when the male line of the Burnell family died out in 1420, the castle was eventually abandoned and fell into the atmospheric weathered ruin visible today.

OPPOSITE: Construction of Ludlow Castle, Shropshire, began in the late eleventh century as the border stronghold of one of the first Marcher lords, Roger de Lacy. Ludlow's transformation from a functional fortress into a royal palace dates from the early fourteenth century, when Roger Mortimer shrewdly married into the family that owned the castle. Its sheer size and scale present a magnificent spectacle when viewed from a distance, its long history reflected in the Norman, medieval and Tudor architecture extant in the high curtain walls and buildings encased within them. The seat of the Council of the Marches, Ludlow Castle also saw tragedy on a personal and human scale. It was from here that the 'Princes in the Tower' were taken to London for 'safe keeping'. Henry VII's elder son, Prince Arthur, died prematurely at Ludlow, leaving his brother to inherit the throne as Henry VIII and marry his widow, Catherine of Aragon.

RIGHT: Wigmore Castle, Herefordshire, was associated with the powerful Mortimer dynasty for nearly four centuries; it was one of the main fortresses from which they controlled large parts of central Wales and the Marches. The surviving ruins date from the thirteenth and fourteenth centuries. Having remained virtually untouched since it was abandoned in the seventeenth century, it is a significant archaeological resource, with deposits of earth up to 4 metres deep and the buildings of its inner bailey buried up to first-floor level. Since taking over guardianship of the site, English Heritage has arrested the castle's decline. Repairs to standing fabric have been applied with a very light touch simply to render it safe, rather than try to reconstitute walls and towers as they might once have appeared. Archaeologists will be kept deliriously happy for many years by this most atmospheric of all the ruined Marcher castles.

spring

Spring is by far the most appealing of the seasons: to witness nature's annual process of renewal is a privilege that cannot be overstated. We live in an automated age where shortcuts are the norm and time is always in short supply. Farmers are as hard-pressed by shortages of precious time and labour as any manufacturer, but for them the cycle of birth, growth and harvest has an unwritten timetable that can rarely be manipulated.

Predicting when everything is likely to happen is not an exact science and largely depends on how cold or wet the preceding months have been. Distinctly varied micro-climates prevail within the different sectors of the Welsh Marches. When the daffodils lining the roadside verges between Ludlow and Shrewsbury are in full bloom, their counterparts higher up in the hills near Offa's Dyke might be displaying no more than a few tentative inches of green leaf above ground level. However, regardless of how harsh the winter has been, the hedgerow and woodland flowers will eventually appear, lambs will joyously discover their capability for vertical take-off, and the dark days of winter will soon be a passing memory. As the days gradually begin to lengthen, the countryside sloughs off the drab skin of winter and replaces it with fresh, shiny green.

BELOW: The northern fringes of the Black Mountains viewed from Hay-on-Wye. Even during the most benign days of late spring, when the surrounding countryside is bathed in warm sunlight, the hills more than live up to their name by being shrouded in unrelenting low cloud and mist.

BELOW: Spring lambs silhouetted against a vibrant dusk sky on the Black Mountains were photographed during a brief interlude when the dark clouds swirling around the plateau's bleak expanses briefly relented and lifted for a few seconds.

BELOW: Few vehicles now use the twisting tree-lined lane that winds past Sowdley Wood, high above the Clun Valley, making it an ideal location for a safe nature walk, and you don't have to get your feet wet! Beyond the avenue's mossy verges and native broadleaf species, banks of conifers host birds such as Siskin and Crossbill, whose distinctive chatter resonates through the trees.

RIGHT: Immediately to the west of Craven Arms, an old Roman road forms one strand of a geometric network of narrow lanes and bridle tracks, linking isolated farming communities and the villages of Sibdon Carwood and Cheney Longville. The latter was named after Hugh Cheney who, in 1394, was granted the last 'licence to crenellate' to be issued by the crown in Shropshire.

OVERLEAF: Windswept farmland near Offa's Dyke between Presteigne and Knighton.

BELOW: The bridge over the River Arrow at Eardisland was one of several strategically important crossing points on the main routes to Wales. The castle that once protected it has long since disappeared.

OPPOSITE, ABOVE: Shrouded in white cherry blossom, the ancient bridge over the River Lugg at Mortimer's Cross overlooks an eighteenth-century water mill. This river crossing was less serene in February 1461, when it was the site of one of many battles fought between the houses of York and Lancaster in the Wars of the Roses (1455–85).

OPPOSITE, BELOW: Fresh green willow and cherry blossom grow over the banks of the River Arrow at Eardisland, one of the villages that features on the region's 'Black & White Villages Trail'.

ABOVE AND OPPOSITE:
Herefordshire is renowned for its
cider making and in springtime
the apple orchards are awash
with delicately shaded pink and
white blossom. Modern bush
orchards designed for ease
of mechanical harvesting are
inevitably replacing the more
traditional ones of the past,
where animals grazed among
the trees and fruit was picked
by hand. Fortunately, some

independent producers still make
organic cider using techniques
handed down through
generations, being able to call
upon a colourful cast list of
English apple varieties, each with
its own individual characteristics.
How could one fail to enjoy a
cider created from varieties such
as Broxwood Foxwhelp, Porters
Perfection, Stoke Red, Brown
Snout, Dabinett, White Norman
or Chisel Jersey?

OPPOSITE, ABOVE: Wild flowers such as violets (left) and red campion (right) bring welcome colour to a predominately green landscape of woodland, fields and hedgerows.

OPPOSITE, BELOW: Vibrant yellow gorse (left) looks appealing from a distance but its sharp barbs make a formidable foe to the walker when inadvertently encountered at close quarters. Cherry blossom (right) is becoming an increasingly prevalent feature in hedgerows and managed woodlands, as landowners expand their planting regimes to include a wider spectrum of native tree species into the countryside.

RIGHT: Bluebells are unquestionably beautiful flowers in their own right, but when massed together and set amid the fresh green of beech trees in spring, they create an unforgettable barrage of colour.

OPPOSITE, ABOVE: *The carefully spaced avenue of trees in the parkland at Shobdon is colourfully juxtaposed with the solid adjacent mass of vibrant yellow oilseed rape.*

OPPOSITE, BELOW: *Broadleaf woodlands may appear to be entirely natural in their conformation, but to sustain them properly requires a constant programme of skilled management. Individual trees need room to thrive and older specimens require selective lopping to ensure their ability to withstand the rigours of winter gales.*

RIGHT: *Renovations and extensions may have prolonged the life of this half-timbered farmhouse but, despite the grants and subsidies now available to hill farmers and smallholders in the border region, making a decent living from the land is still far from easy.*

RIGHT: The mumming tradition may not be the force it was, but still survives in the same way that folk songs and oral storytelling have done – passed on from generation to generation in families that value these integral parts of our cultural heritage. George and the Dragon may be perceived as pure pantomime, but it has historical links with the medieval Crusades.

BELOW: Each May Day Bank Holiday weekend, Ludlow's historic market square and surrounding streets reverberate with the raucous noise of a modern funfair.

OPPOSITE: Clun's Green Man festival is one of a dwindling number in England to celebrate the ancient pagan rites of spring. The annual ritual of the Green Man begins at the church before progressing to the village's fourteenth-century bridge. The 'hero' there encounters the Ice Queen of winter and her cohorts and, after a good deal of posturing and shouting but with no actual violence, spring gains the day. The victory is celebrated in traditional rural style by much thirst-quenching and toasting!

historic inns

Many of the historic hotels that still play an important role in town and village life date back to their days as coaching inns, with some of the oldest establishments having evolved from monastic hospices. The history of coaching inns is inseparable from the development of the English road network, and it was not until the introduction of the first Turnpike Act in 1663 that long-distance travel gradually became more commonplace.

By the 1750s, vast improvements in road conditions and carriage design saw a rapid increase in the volume of traffic, but the distance a coach could cover in any one stage was still limited by the stamina of the horses, and was usually 20–25km/ 12–15 miles. Coaching inns therefore sprang up along all the main routes, to provide teams of fresh animals for the next leg of a journey and food or overnight accommodation for the passengers. Some of the larger inns became renowned as social meeting places for the upper echelons of society, hosting lavish events in glittering ballrooms. Towards the 1830s, some inns became even more extravagant, adding huge porticoes to their facades as an indication of perceived importance. But, having burned so brightly towards the end, the flame of the coaching era was almost instantly snuffed out by the arrival of the rail-ways after the 1830s. Many inns simply went out of business, others survived by running hire services to and from the nearest rail station, and many remained dormant until awakened by the welcome sound of the internal combustion engine and a new era of road travel.

OPPOSITE, ABOVE LEFT: Despite its name, the New Inn in Pembridge, Herefordshire, is reputed to be one of the oldest in the county, dating back to the early seventeenth century; there was probably an alehouse on the site before that. Originally a farmhouse, the inn is close to Pembridge's medieval open market hall, and its history of hospitality probably began with the farmer selling home-brewed ale to the wool merchants who congregated near his premises. With the advent of coach transport, the New Inn became a notable staging post on the route to and from Wales; a measure of its importance is highlighted by the fact that for many years it housed the local court.

OPPOSITE, ABOVE RIGHT: The Rhydspence Inn in Whitney-on-Wye, Herefordshire, was originally a fourteenth-century manor house. Two centuries later, it had become an important inn and assembly point on a drove road from Wales known as the Black Ox Trail, letting out grazing land for livestock before they continued their journey to the English markets. The boundary between England and Wales runs through its garden. The Victorian diarist Rev. Francis Kilvert noted, as he rode eastwards one night, 'the English inn still ablaze with light and the song of revellers, but the Welsh inn was dark and still'. The Methodist-inspired Welsh temperance movement ground to a halt at the Rhydspence.

LEFT: Although by no means a unique occurrence, the naming of a town after its pub is far from commonplace! The Craven Arms coaching inn was built at the junction in Shropshire where the route to Wales via Clun branches off the main Shrewsbury to Ludlow road. It was named after the Earls of Craven, owners of nearby Stokesay Castle. The town of the same name began to develop during the railway era, when the inn became a vital hub for local sheep farmers. They drove animals down from the hills into one of the largest stockyards in the country, from where they could be transported to markets far afield. It is sad, however, that renovations to the old Craven Arms have deprived it of the atmosphere and sense of history that it once had.

OPPOSITE: The exuberant black-and-white facade of the Dragon Hotel in Montgomery, Montgomeryshire, resembles the bench in a piano maker's workshop! This ancient inn occupies a prominent position above the market square and old town hall, shadowed by a steep escarpment crowned by the ruined castle. The town used to be the administrative centre for the county, and during its heyday in the early nineteenth century the inn welcomed passengers from The Dart express coach. It also accommodated the executioner tasked with performing the town's last public hanging.

BELOW: Situated in the heart of medieval Shrewsbury, the Prince Rupert takes its name from King Charles I's nephew, who lived in the building around the time of the English Civil War. The Royalists' inspirational General of the Horse, he was the architect of many of his side's most notable victories, but his impetuosity and tactical naivety also contributed to several crucial defeats. The hotel has been meticulously restored under the guidance of historical and conservation experts from English Heritage. It incorporates Shrewsbury's oldest secular building, the twelfth-century Mansion House. There is always a worry that places with such a pedigree as the Prince Rupert will be manipulated for commercial gain and present a dreaded 'olde worlde' facade. Happily, this particular slice of hospitality history remains untarnished – Rupert himself would happily shrug off his armour and feel quite at home.

BELOW: The Lion Hotel in Shrewsbury, Shropshire, is definitely the doyen of all the surviving Marches coaching inns and, apart from motor traffic, its surroundings have probably changed little over time. Shrewsbury was an important staging post on the routes between Chester, north Wales and the Midlands. The building is mostly eighteenth century around a much earlier core; it was one of Shrewsbury's most important social centres, with elegant assembly rooms and a vast ballroom. It is recorded that the legendary violinist Paganini gave a recital here in 1831; exactly a quarter of a century later, author Charles Dickens enthralled guests with one of his public readings. One can still get a sense of the scale of its operation as a coaching inn. The old stable and coaching yard now serves as the hotel garage; it can still be accessed through a low arch to one side of the main entrance.

THESE PAGES: The elaborate timber facade of The Feathers in Ludlow, Shropshire, is justifiably world-famous. No matter how many times one views it, hitherto unnoticed details seem literally to emerge out of the woodwork. The Feathers was built as a house in 1619 by Rees Jones, a wealthy local lawyer who had no doubt prospered from the presence in Ludlow of the Council of the Marches. Many parts of the Marches sided with the Royalist cause during the English Civil War, and Jones's son Thomas served as a captain in the king's army. He converted the family house to an inn around 1670. The choice of name was fairly common in the region: feathers referred to the ostrich plumes that formed the Prince of Wales's insignia – in most cases (and certainly in the case of Ludlow) it marked a retrospective celebration of the investiture as Prince of the future King Charles I in 1616. During the mid eighteenth century, the inn flourished as an important posting house, stabling around a hundred horses at any one time; it was even reputed to have had its own cockpit. The building comprises three storeys, each with three bays and gables. The balcony was added later during nineteenth-century restorations, and was subsequently used for electioneering speeches.

half-timbered buildings

Timber-framed houses are an integral part of the landscape in some areas of the Marches, so much so that one can now follow a signposted 'Black & White Villages Trail' around Herefordshire. The starkness of some of these buildings can be quite disconcerting, but in most cases the famous 'magpie' effect originates from the aesthetically unfortunate nineteenth-century practice of treating exposed timbers with black bitumen and covering the infill with whitewashed plaster.

In regions of England where trees were plentiful but decent building stone difficult to extract, transport and dress, timber-framed houses were a practical and economically viable alternative. The term 'half-timbering' means that the logs were split into two lengthwise rather than being used as whole tree trunks (as in cruck frames). Oak was the most commonly used wood, and the large number of centuries-old buildings that are still habitable today is a testament to its durability, although many have floors and stairs difficult to negotiate due to the wood's natural warping. Standard-sized vernacular dwellings were often prefabricated and erected on site, the skeletal timber box resting on a stone or brick footing. Upper storeys were added by simply placing another appropriately supported box on top of the ground-floor frame. The panels were filled initially with wattle and daub, and later with either brick or stone.

Regional variations on the basic technique create different visual effects around the country. Shropshire and Herefordshire usually display square infill panels, whereas East Anglian craftsmen favoured close studding, in which the frame is divided into narrow, vertical panels. This system was employed on some of the more prestigious Marches buildings from the fifteenth century onwards – perhaps more as a cosmetic status symbol than a technical advance, to show off how much expensive timber the owner could afford. Another device used by the wealthy to set their properties apart was the addition of elaborately carved, non-functional panels, struts or beams. The Feathers in Ludlow is an extreme example, illustrating how far a determined property-owner could go if so motivated.

As with all natural products, timber is a finite resource unless it is properly managed and replaced. By the seventeenth century, dwindling supplies, coupled with an increasing requirement for ships as Britain expanded as a maritime power, placed heavy additional demands on oak forests. Brick had been introduced from the Low Countries during the late medieval period, but for many years it had been considered a luxury item available only to those at the upper end of the social and economic scale. As domestic production increased, however, brick became more widely available. In many parts of the Marches, it was even used to replace the traditional plaster infill on timber-framed buildings. Because it had no structural role when used in this way, quite elaborate herringbone patterns were used to create the panels. The distinctive combination of weathered brick and timber is, to this day, extremely aesthetically appealing.

LEFT: Weobley is one of Herefordshire's best-known black-and-white villages and has some impressive individual examples of timber-framed buildings, including the fourteenth-century Red Lion pub. From some viewpoints the village almost resembles the vision of rural England portrayed in many early Hollywood films, but the steady flow of traffic and parking restriction notices confirm it is real enough. By far the best time to explore Weobley is towards evening, when the glaringly white walls are suffused with the softer, mellow colours of sunset.

BELOW: The visual effect of colour-washed plaster against naturally ageing timber can be so much more aesthetically pleasing than stark black-and-white. The upper floor of this house near Weobley, Herefordshire, protrudes further out than the ground level, thereby providing some protection against rain and foul weather in the days before guttering and downpipes were commonplace.

BELOW, RIGHT: Despite phases of restoration, the ancient Guildhall in Much Wenlock, Shropshire, manages to combine the atmosphere of centuries past with the dignity of ongoing civic service. The building served as a courthouse from 1540 until 1895, and the first floor is still regularly used for town council meetings. The dark-stained timbers and whitewashed infill need to be painted carefully with a steady hand: mistakes are rather difficult to hide or successfully retouch.

OVERLEAF: Many medieval villages radiate outwards from the nucleus of a church or castle, but Pembridge, Herefordshire, has developed in a linear fashion along either side of the main Leominster to Aberystwyth road. This row of terraced cottages perfectly illustrates how timber-framed buildings warp and settle with age, though seldom with any serious threat to their safety or stability. As one looks along the terrace as a whole, it is extraordinary to observe the pronounced undulations of the upper-floor timbers and also how some dwellings have been constructed on significantly higher stone plinths than their neighbours. They could well have been made that way to combat the mud and debris thrown up by passing horses, carts and carriages during the long, wet winter months and to minimise the damage that might result from the flooding of the adjacent River Arrow.

BELOW: Not all the buildings in Pembridge, Herefordshire, are black-and-white: this pair provides an interesting contrast. The cottages on the left look as though they have been renovated with brick infill to replace the panels' original material. The larger property on the right seems to have retained most of its original structure, with a jettied gable end. Although the device of close studding was sometimes cosmetic, larger houses benefited from the load-bearing capabilities of extra timbers. The weight of a large slate roof had to be dissipated down through the structure as evenly as possible, rather than relying on just a few major stress points.

ABOVE AND RIGHT: Stokesay's enchanting half-timbered gatehouse was a later addition to the castle and patently not intended as a serious defensive structure, although attackers might have been temporarily delayed by pausing to admire the craftsmanship. Completed some time around the early seventeenth century, it is a well-preserved example of the lavishly carved timber-framing that was undergoing something of a renaissance during the late Elizabethan era. Almost every exposed surface is covered with elaborate detail, either decorative scrollwork or more complex representations of biblical themes, including a portrayal of events in the Garden of Eden.

OPPOSITE: Since World War One, poppies have become synonymous with those slain in battle. This field of vibrant red flowers was found, appropriately, by the banks of the River Severn near to the site of the bloody Battle of Shrewsbury, fought on 21 July 1403. There, a rebel army led by Henry 'Hotspur' Percy of Northumberland was routed by the forces of the Lancastrian king, Henry IV.

summer

The summer months are a busy time for everybody in the Welsh Marches; as daylight hours increase and temperatures rise, plant and animal growth – both natural and cultivated – accelerates. Flowers turn to buds in preparation for the annual harvest of fruit and vegetables for humans, nuts and seeds for wildlife. The roads also gradually start to fill with cars, as people travel from far afield to savour one of Britain's most unspoilt areas, and therein lies the conundrum of tourism. When a place is visited and admired for its tranquillity, there comes a point when the noise of vehicles and people drowns out the silence.

Fortunately, the Welsh Marches have more than enough country lanes, footpaths and bridleways to assimilate a number of visitors before their presence becomes any kind of intrusion, especially since the Countryside Act came into force in 2000, opening up even more areas of the landscape to public access. Those who derive their living from the countryside have adapted to increased tourism by providing farmhouse accommodation and selling food whose taste is a revelation to supermarket-reared guests.

BELOW: A field of ripening barley photographed shortly after sunrise above Herefordshire's Golden Valley. The warm colours and textures of the landscape created by the sun's low angle at that time of day provide ample compensation for having to be up and on location at such an early hour!

OPPOSITE: The first early summer cut of sileage marks the start of the harvesting season in the countryside. While fields of cereal crops are still raw and green, the grass is cut and collected in large tractor-drawn trailers that maintain a non-stop shuttle service to and from the farm. The operation often goes on into the night since fine, dry days are a precious commodity that cannot be wasted.

BELOW: The view from the top of Clun's castle mound highlights what a commanding position it held, giving the occupants a clear view of any impending threat materialising from the surrounding countryside.

OPPOSITE: The Royal Oak pub in Cardington lies in the shadow of Caer Caradoc, to the east of Church Stretton; it is a perfect example of the archetypal English country pub. Set at the foot of a steep hill amid a confusing labyrinth of narrow, high-banked lanes, the ancient inn is dominated by the tower of the parish church of St James.

OPPOSITE: Wild or 'dog' roses (above left) enrich the hedgerows of early summer with delicate pink flowers that, later in the year, will be transformed into rosehips, the red berries that make a valuable contribution to nature's complex food chain. Rhododendrons (above right) have spread rapidly from prized cultivated specimens to rampant woodland shrubs.

RIGHT: Although not a common feature within the Marches landscape, banked field boundaries are yet another invaluable habitat for wildlife, providing food and shelter for small rodents and birds.

LEFT: The forestry road leading up to the Water-Break-its-Neck falls in Radnor Forest makes that spectacular natural feature more accessible to many visitors who might otherwise have struggled to gain access across the rough woodland and scrub terrain.

BELOW: The River Teme near Bringewood Forge, Bromfield, an area far more tranquil than back in the seventeenth and eighteenth centuries, when the river supplied water-power to a nearby iron smelting site.

OPPOSITE: Queenswood Country Park near Hereford covers over 40 ha/100 acres of semi-natural ancient woodland that have been designated as a Site of Special Scientific Interest (SSSI) and also as a Local Nature Reserve (LNR). At the heart of the site is an arboretum containing over 500 rare or exotic trees.

THESE PAGES: Vast tracts of the Welsh Marches are given over to sheep farming; although some of the upland areas are comprised of scrub and poor pastures, much of the land seldom exceeds 500m/1,600ft in height and consequently produces plenty of rich grazing. Summer shearing is a hectic time as the scattered flocks have to be rounded up and brought down from the hillsides. Llanfair Hill (opposite) is a typical example of sheep territory; although the farmers find it easier to get around on modern quad bikes, their wiry, hard-working dogs more than earn their keep.

OVERLEAF: The River Teme from Lingen Bridge. Although a 40-km/25-mile stretch of the River Teme marks the border between England and Wales, Lingen Bridge crosses it just a few hundred yards before it becomes a national boundary. Extensive beds of River Water Crowfoot evoke memories of childhood picnics, flimsy fishing nets and jam-jars suspended on lengths of string in which to carry home in triumph any unfortunate minnows or sticklebacks caught hiding in the weed beds.

OPPOSITE:The annual Ludlow Festival takes place during the last week in June and the first in July. The event's focal point is an open-air presentation of a William Shakespeare play, performed against the atmospheric backdrop of the town's historic castle. This photograph shows the 2005 production of 'Richard II', directed by Steven Berkoff.

BELOW: Hay-on-Wye, long known as the world's largest second-hand bookshop, has also now established a reputation for hosting one of the country's most popular and prestigious literary festivals at the beginning of June. However, despite the summer schedule, meteorological stability is not one of the Welsh Marches' strong points!

BELOW: Many of the fields of the Marches are still encompassed by traditional hedges, commonplace throughout the countryside before 'prairie' farming practices rendered small areas less profitable. With every grubbed-out hedgerow, another priceless wildlife habitat and food store is lost forever.

OPPOSITE: Advances in farm machine technology have rendered the old rectangular straw bale virtually redundant. Harvested fields are now strewn with larger and heavier round versions that can only be lifted by mechanical means, although many smaller farms with steep terrain to manage persist with the old method of collecting and storing baled straw.

BELOW AND OPPOSITE: As summer draws to a close, the swathes of green bracken covering wide expanses of hills such as the Long Mynd start to wilt and discolour, before transforming the landscape into a rich golden brown for the duration of winter. A rapacious plant, it poses a serious threat to the purple heather we take for granted as an integral part of the countryside's annual display of colour. Many people are absolutely opposed to country pursuits such as grouse shooting, but without the constant management of the grouse's natural habitat of heather, bracken will spread unchecked – ultimately it would envelop and destroy the heather forever.

marcher towns

Theoretically, a Marcher town can be any of those located within the broad corridor of the Welsh Marches. However, the term tends to be used more specifically to describe the major garrisons or administrative centres established initially by William I in the eleventh century to aid his subjugation of the fiercely independent Welsh. Shrewsbury and Hereford were two of the three earldoms he created (Chester was the third), and those power bases became instrumental in the centuries-long struggle for Wales that continued through the reigns of a succession of English monarchs. But it was a smaller town, Ludlow, which became the absolute centre of power in the region. Ludlow's fortress belonged to the Mortimer dynasty; it later housed the Council of Wales and the Welsh Marches, effectively transforming it into the capital of Wales.

BELOW: Shrewsbury is almost completely encircled by a teardrop-shaped loop of the River Severn; although it is served by several crossing places, the English and Welsh bridges are the two main road links. The English Bridge, shown here, was the main point of access: an elegant, balustraded structure built in 1770. In 1920, it was the subject of a complex restoration project. With motor traffic becoming the norm, the bridge was deemed too steep and narrow. It was meticulously dismantled, piece by piece, widened by some 26 feet and then rebuilt with a slightly shallower gradient.

RIGHT: Narrow Lane, Wyle Cop, Shrewsbury. The curiously named Wyle Cop is the road that runs up into the ancient heart of Shrewsbury from the English Bridge. It is thought to be derived from two Welsh words: 'hwylfa' (road up a hillside) and 'coppa' (top or head). The area is interlaced with narrow passageways known as shuts; although some provide shortcuts from one main thoroughfare to another, many – frustratingly for anyone unfamiliar with the network – turn out to be no more than atmospheric cul-de-sacs.

FAR RIGHT: Rowley's House, Shrewsbury. William Rowley, a prosperous draper, brewer and one-time mayor of Shrewsbury, built this magnificent half-timbered warehouse; it now houses a local museum. Rowley was also responsible for the brick mansion that adjoins it: completed in 1618, it was recorded as the first dwelling in the town to be constructed entirely of that material. Despite the obvious architectural and historical value of the two buildings, they might not survive development plans for the area. Naturally, there is much opposition to these proposals.

RIGHT: The Abbot's House, Butcher Row, Shrewsbury. Butcher Row is one of the narrow streets in the Bear Steps complex of Tudor Shrewsbury. It leads on to Fish Street, where the fresh meat and fish merchants plied their trade. The Abbot's House is the end house in a row built by Lilleshall Abbey in 1458, but there is no record of an abbot ever having lived in it. The buildings comprised a ground-floor shop fronting the street, with private chambers above. It could have been an early buy-to-let venture, with the rent providing valuable income for the abbey. An official opening ceremony in 1459 was attended by the Abbot of Lilleshall and borough officials. The monks might well have approved of the current merchandise on offer in the Abbot's House, though they might have felt obliged to say otherwise.

BELOW: As Broad Street climbs steadily upwards from Ludlow's medieval walls, the variety of architectural styles on view perfectly encapsulates Ludlow's growth and social history. The church and lavish half-timbered shops and inns clustered around the market place at the top of Broad Street reflect wealth accumulated from the Middle Ages through the wool and cloth industries. Retail and hospitality flourished further due to trade generated by the Council of the Marches, although there was a decline in the town's fortunes when this was abolished in 1689. The setback was merely temporary, since glove-making then became Ludlow's main industry. Successful manufacturers, traders and other professional classes built elegant Georgian brick houses and larger mansions below the black-and-white Tudor enclave. One of the most impressive of those original buildings was the Angel Inn. Although it no longer functions as an inn, the almost surreal display of two glittering, angelic mannequins in a first-floor bay window are reminders of its place in Ludlow's history.

RIGHT: The pink sandstone tower of Ludlow's magnificent parish church soars to over 40m/130 feet, dominating the town skyline and creating a memorable landmark from the surrounding countryside. Most of the church dates to the fifteenth century, and the tower certainly surpasses the grandeur of many of Suffolk's great 'wool churches'. The interior is equally splendid, with soaring angels adorning the chancel roof and a superb collection of carved misericords in the choir stalls. Most depict scenes from medieval life and, in common with similar collections, one or two display a degree of artistic licence, incorporating the odd bawdy scene that seems inappropriate to the ecclesiastical setting. If one has a sound heart and not too nervous a disposition, the tower can be climbed via a narrow and claustrophobic stone staircase that winds interminably upwards. The view from the top is ample reward for one's exertions, but the descent is equally demanding – a firm grip on the thick guide rope is strongly advised.

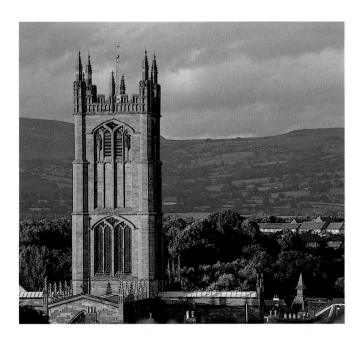

RIGHT: The fifteenth-century bridge over the River Wye and Hereford's exquisite cathedral harmoniously combine to create an image of peace and tranquillity. However, it was not always thus. Having been seized from the Welsh, Hereford became the capital of the Saxon kingdom of West Mercia and for centuries was at the forefront of Anglo–Welsh border conflicts. The See of Hereford dates from 676 AD, but the Saxon cathedral was destroyed in 1055; the oldest parts of the present structure date back to the late eleventh century. The Norman bishop, Robert de Losinga, was the builder, and examples of his impressive work survive in the columns and arches of the nave and choir. Hereford's stunning architecture is often overlooked by visitors intent on viewing only the cathedral's twin treasures of its chained library and the Mappa Mundi. Research has dated the extraordinary vellum map of the known world to around 1300: its creator, Richard of Haldingham, showed Jerusalem at the centre, with everywhere radiating outwards from the keystone of the medieval Church.

villages of the marches

The social structure of the Welsh Marches was affected by the Conquest to a far greater degree than other parts of the Normans' new domain, both in human terms and those of the built environment. Most of the villages of England and Wales that exist today did so before 1066 and, as with other cross-Channel invaders from earlier periods, most of the ordinary French who stayed were simply assimilated into existing communities. The Marches were somewhat different: several villages were newly planned, or developed around the stone castles built by the new lords of the manor. Many Welsh and English settlements remained quite untouched by all the turmoil, although one suspects that taxes were probably increased to high levels to pay for all the new building. Annual fiscal demands were no doubt resented as much then, when delivered by a knight in chainmail bearing a sword, as they are today when appearing in a brown envelope from the postman!

OPPOSITE: From Old Radnor's steep, north-west-facing hillside, the ground falls away to a fertile flood plain created by tributaries of the River Lugg, before climbing up again towards the bleak expanses of Radnor Forest. The tactical reasons for replacing 'Old' with 'New' are readily apparent when the village is viewed from the churchyard: the large area any garrison would need to monitor nullified the advantage of height. The parish church of Old Radnor is dedicated to the first Christian martyr, St Stephen, although this might have been a mistake of interpretation by the Normans: it is likely that the church's original dedication was to the seventh-century Welsh saint, Ystyffan.

OPPOSITE: New Radnor was created in 1064 by Earl Harold Godwinsson (the future King Harold) just two years before his ill-fated encounter with William, Duke of Normandy, at the Battle of Hastings. The site had been chosen to act as a stronghold commanding a major cross-border route; the prefix 'New' simply referred to the fact that it was replacing the nearby settlement of Old Radnor in that role. The Normans obviously agreed with Harold's strategic assessment and proceeded to develop the site further as they sought to establish a foothold in the turbulent Welsh Marches. They laid the village out in a neat grid-iron pattern, with three main streets crossed at right angles by five lanes, all enclosed within a protective wall accessed through four gates. Although most of the village's buildings are now relatively new, the original layout has been retained. The encircling walls have long disappeared, but from the vantage point of the castle mound, their original line can be identified by the grassy banks running to the south and west of the village.

RIGHT: The quiet, laid-back atmosphere that pervades New Radnor in the twenty-first century was not always present. This used to be the county town of Radnorshire (created following the Act of Union with Wales in 1536), and remained a borough until 1886. Traces of that legacy survive through buildings such as the old town hall, and the Eagle Hotel which now stands on the site once occupied by the prison. But the most visually arresting monument to that era stands at the junction of two of Radnor's main streets. The huge, elaborate memorial to Sir George Cornewall Lewis – a collection of gargoyles, arches, pillars and shields with Sir George's white marble profile occupying only a small area – would not be disgraced architecturally if set beside Queen Victoria's tribute to Prince Albert in London's Kensington Gardens. Sir George was New Radnor's MP from 1855 until his death in 1863 and also held high office in Palmerston's government, serving as Chancellor of the Exchequer, Home Secretary and Minister for War.

LEFT: Bishop's Castle is one of those delightful Shropshire communities that was once a bustling town but now has a village-sized population. Its origins go back centuries before the Normans arrived to when the local landowner Egwin 'Shakehead' was apparently cured of his palsy at St Ethelbert's shrine in the Saxon Hereford cathedral. His gratitude knew no bounds, and he allegedly bequeathed his lands to the bishop. When the Normans arrived, they made full use of Egwin's gift. A castle was built on high ground to the west of the Long Mynd ridge and the town gradually grew up around the fortress, radiating down the slope towards the current parish church at the foot of the hill. It was governed by the Bishops of Hereford and their successors until the sixteenth century, when all vestiges of the Marcher lordships' powers were finally stripped away by the Laws in Wales Acts of 1535–42. It is quite a climb up the main street but well worth the effort, as most of the historic Tudor and Elizabethan buildings are clustered near the top. One is known as the House on Crutches due to its overhanging upper storey being supported on posts, beneath which runs a very uneven cobbled thoroughfare.

OPPOSITE BELOW: Clun is the most historically important among the cluster of villages and hamlets whose names reflect their close proximity to the river of the same name. The poetry of A. E. Housman is irrevocably linked to the Welsh Marches and one of the better-known verses from his epic, 'A Shropshire Lad', perfectly sums up the atmosphere of this valley:

Clunton and Clunbury,
Clungunford and Clun
Are the quietest places
Under the sun.

The village grew up around the Saxon church to the south of the river but, following the Conquest, the Normans established a new settlement near their castle on the north bank. Saxon and Norman Clun are linked by a fourteenth-century packhorse bridge – according to local folklore, 'whoever crosses Clun Bridge comes back sharper than he went'. Unfortunately, no clues are offered as to the most advantageous direction of travel!

BELOW: The small community of Brampton Bryan in the far north-west corner of Herefordshire straddles the main road link from Ludlow into Wales. The village's most arresting feature is the ancient yew hedge of Brampton Bryan Hall, home of the Harley family since 1309. This vast, undulating, evergreen sculpture seems belittled by the term 'hedge'. Its annual trimming must be something of a logistical nightmare. This yew barrier performs its job well, completely obscuring any views of the present mansion or the ruins of the castle that preceded it until it was sacked during the Civil War in 1644. As Parliamentarians in a largely Royalist county, Sir Robert Harley and his family were the object of much hostile attention. When the conflict began, Harley's wife – the appropriately named Brilliana – was left in charge of the estates while her husband was on government duty in London. The siege of Brampton Bryan began on 25 July 1643 and lasted for over six weeks; it was unsuccessful, but Brilliana fell ill shortly afterwards and died on 31 October, aged only 43. The castle was finally sacked in 1644 but, as the Royalist cause was lost two years later, Sir Robert was able to claim the not insubstantial sum of £13,000 in compensation.

autumn

As the winding down of another year gets under way, most of the crops have been harvested, but nature stages a final flourish. Hips, haws and blackberries provide much-needed food for birds, animals and those humans who still make use of the fruits of the hedgerow. Long after the cereal harvest has finished, the fruit farmers and cider apple growers begin to gather in their crops. It is sad how few native varieties of apple are available in supermarkets, but village shops and roadside stalls still sell fruit that seems to come from a bygone era. Farmers' markets also play an increasingly important role in these rural economies: amid stalls of meat, fruit and vegetables, jars of homemade jams and preserves bear testimony to the continuity of a traditional way of life. The wide expanses of the upland moors settle into a uniform brown as heather and bracken lose their vibrant purple and green. It is easy to forget that such seemingly natural environments need careful management to be maintained. Bracken is a rapacious plant: unless checked, it will gradually swamp the more visually appealing but less robust heather. The skilful and frequently unnoticed contributions of conservationists, forestry workers and gamekeepers help to sustain the moors and woodlands that form such an important part of the British landscape.

BELOW: Herefordshire's Golden Valley did not originally derive its name through any connection with that colour but, on a mellow sunlit autumnal day, it certainly lives up to its description. The vibrant red soil being turned over by the tractor and plough combine with the tyre tracks and the field's yellow stubble to create a strong graphic image, accentuated by the condensing effect of a telephoto lens.

OPPOSITE: The flanks of the Black Mountains near Llanthony Priory give another example of how invaluable a telephoto lens is in landscape photography. By finding an elevated vantage point, zooming in on a small section of a panorama and completely excluding any sky, one is able to create a powerful image by utilising textures, lines and colours that might go unnoticed in a wider view of the same scene.

LEFT: *The view from Old Radnor churchyard reveals a pattern of field systems that have remained unchanged for centuries. The extensive use of high, cultivated hedges, punctuated by mature trees, creates a natural windbreak, protecting crops and livestock from the potentially destructive gales that can whip through the valley.*

RIGHT: *The River Wye at Symond's Yat is one of the finest river views in England or Wales. Although slightly further south than the geographical parameters of the Marches defined in this book, its sheer beauty demanded its inclusion! The Wye was the first major river to be designated as a Site of Special Scientific Interest (SSSI) along its entire length; below Hereford it has also been afforded the status of an Area of Outstanding Natural Beauty (AONB).*

BELOW: The Severn Bridge at Atcham was built on the site of the original ford where the river is broad and shallow, necessitating a longer bridge than might have been expected. It was built by John Gwynn between 1769 and 1771, who was also responsible for designing the English Bridge in Shrewsbury.

BELOW: Autumn in Montgomery may alter the colour of its immediate environs, but little else seems to change with the passing of time in this tranquil border town. It could have been designed with photography in mind: the cluster of buildings around the town hall, the church and distant Shropshire Hills are perfectly juxtaposed to create a portrait of countryside that should be treasured and never taken for granted.

OVERLEAF: The Shropshire Hills near Church Stretton by moonlight was a photograph that almost did not get taken. I was cold, tired and facing a three-hour drive home, but the image was so evocative it could not be ignored. It was quite dark, and my concern was that the sheep would keep moving during the necessarily long exposure. I was able to keep blurring to a minimum by patiently waiting until the sheep transferred to a new piece of grass on which to put their heads down and graze.

LEFT AND BELOW: The renowned eighteenth-century landscape designer Humphrey Repton was commissioned to create a scheme for Attingham Park in 1797, and much of his original layout remains intact today. Numerous ancient trees, especially oaks, are just about hanging on to life – as with all trees, they become such an integral part of the landscape for so many years that their demise leaves a massive visual vacuum. The replanting and regeneration of woodland or individual specimens is a long-term process, and regardless of how attractive any thriving young trees may appear they inevitably lack the character of their elderly peers.

LEFT: The red sandstone of Shrewsbury Abbey acquires an even mellower shade when touched by the late autumn sun. The site originally housed a small Saxon church, replaced by the great Benedictine abbey founded by Roger de Montgomery, a relative of William the Conqueror, in 1083. Although much was lost at the time of the Dissolution, the abbey church's nave has survived and now serves as a particularly sumptuous parish church.

BELOW: A rapidly descending sun creates deep pools of shadow across the distinctive ridges of the Long Mynd. The dark foreground is relieved by the few strands of bracken just catching a glimmer of light.

OPPOSITE: The autumnal colour shift in the landscape is an unpredictable event and no two years are likely to follow the same pattern of transformation. I was particularly fortunate to have the advantage of height for this shot of woods near Goodrich Castle, in which just about every available shade of nature's palette is on display.

BELOW: When viewed from the Stiperstones ridge, the Long Mynd's west-facing aspect appears far less intimidating than when encountered at closer quarters. September can be a good month for landscape photography, as the presence of colours other than the ubiquitous green help give greater depth and definition to an image.

OPPOSITE: Most of the Golden Valley's villages are worthy of exploration and Vowchurch is no exception. On crisp, clear days, the distant Black Mountains appear deceptively close and one can trace the course of every stream and gully cascading down the massif's eastern ridge. The church's diminutive bell tower is its most appealing exterior feature, but the interior is remarkable for the early seventeenth-century roof reconstruction, in which nave and chancel were supported by huge carved oak posts.

OPPOSITE: The colours of the countryside in autumn are perfect for detailed photographic studies and specialist equipment is not necessarily required to capture nature's glorious handiwork. Dew-laden cobwebs benefit from back-lighting to show off their intricate construction, and the Shaggy Ink Cap looks far more appealing in its infancy than a few days later when the cap is reduced to a dark, slimy mass.

BELOW: As the temperature drops rapidly after sunset, mist quickly forms just above the surface of fields and watercourses. For a brief period, there is sufficient light in the western sky to allow it to be photographed as a tangible entity. An elevated position is crucial to give the swirling fingers of mist and the receding lines of trees sufficient depth.

churches of the marches

The churches of the Welsh Marches cannot readily be grouped into clearly defined categories, due to the region's diverse historical development, its fluctuating centres of population and the variations in its architectural styles and building materials from county to county. Two of the greatest influences were the Normans and, several centuries later, the Victorians.

William I and his cohorts were devout Christians and deeply religious. After terrorising the Saxon population and establishing their security behind stone castle walls, they set about building churches with equal vigour. The Romanesque style of architecture they imported has survived throughout England, with the Marches boasting some of the finest examples of the genre in its purest form. The Victorians had an even greater influence on the parish church, and many rural villages were subjected to the well-intentioned, but far too heavy, hand of restoration. It can be a great disappointment to see places where domestic medieval buildings have survived in their original form, but where the local church has been architecturally sanitised.

One has to venture deeper into Wales to savour the real ethos of Welsh Nonconformism through the chapels that contrast so markedly with English parish churches. Fortunately, there are some excellent examples within sight of Offa's Dyke. It would be fascinating to travel back in time to experience the 'fire and brimstone' days of early Methodism as opposed to the more measured tones of the Anglican church. In this more secular age, neither is flourishing as well as it might, but regardless of whether or not people fill the ancient places of worship they remain impressive and moving testaments to those who built them as enduring acts of faith.

OPPOSITE AND ABOVE:
St Mary and St David, Kilpeck, Herefordshire, is arguably the finest surviving example of a small Norman church in England, with a quite remarkable array of Romanesque decoration. Although the centre of the tympanum above the south door features the Tree of Life (opposite), many of the surrounding figures belong more to Celtic mythology and nature than to the more common religious iconography. More than seventy grotesque sculptures form the corbel table that runs round the outside of the church, ranging from human heads to hunting symbols – and some that could have been transposed from the darkest corner of a Hieronymus Bosch painting. Kilpeck is one of several churches in this part of the county to feature almost identical examples of skilled craftsmanship – collectively they have become known as the Herefordshire School of Romanesque sculpture. It is extremely fortuitous that this particular building has been fashioned from a highly durable red sandstone. Churches from this period in other parts of the country made of softer stone have aged badly, their elaborate carved decorations part-dissolving like a seaside sandcastle succumbing to the tide.

RIGHT: St Michael and All Angels, Castle Frome, Herefordshire, boasts a Norman font that is a masterpiece of post-Conquest Romanesque – the finest individual example of the genre within the Herefordshire School. It is a large tub, tapering at the bottom, standing upon a bizarre, crouching, bearded man whose facial expression conveys a distinct lack of enthusiasm for having been forced to bear such a weight for eternity. Between the braided stone borders are depicted the angel, eagle, lion and cow symbols of the four evangelists, with a wonderful portrayal of the baptism of Christ by John the Baptist as the central scene.

LEFT AND BELOW: Langley Chapel, Acton Burnell, Shropshire, lies hidden among fields and narrow lanes in rolling countryside (below). It survives under the guardianship of English Heritage as a perfect example of the manner in which small, rural, Anglican churches were laid out in the early seventeenth century. The original building can be traced back to 1313, when Richard Burnell obtained permission to build a chapel some 9.5km/6 miles south of the family seat at Acton. Original medieval fragments were retained when the chapel was rebuilt around 1546, but Langley's outstanding feature is a complete set of original furnishings belonging to the early seventeenth century (left). The box pews, musicians' desk and benches around the communion table remained in situ due to the fact that the chapel was largely unused from the late seventeenth century, and was therefore spared the subsequent changes in fashion regarding how churches were fitted out.

RIGHT: St Mary, Pembridge, Herefordshire, boasts a fourteenth-century detached belfry – although by no means unique, it is one of only a handful in Herefordshire. The interior is a veritable forest of ancient oak timbers, bracing each other in a Scandinavian building style, occasionally used in East Anglia but rarely this far west. Pembridge occupied a vulnerable position on one of the main routes though the Marches into Wales: the belfry's additional role as a place of refuge is confirmed by numerous narrow embrasures around the tower's lower wall, slits through which defenders could fire arrows down on raiding parties. The word belfry, Germanic in origin, originally referred to movable towers used in medieval sieges.

LEFT AND BELOW: The first known church serving the Shobdon estate in Herefordshire was an Anglo-Saxon timber chapel, which the new, post-Conquest owner, Oliver de Merlimond, decided to replace with a stone structure. During the planning, de Merlimond went on a pilgrimage to Santiago de Compostela, and was so impressed by the Romanesque architecture of northern Spain that he commissioned his own church to be completed in the same style. It was probably the first project undertaken by the twelfth-century masons whose artistry is seen to such good effect in other local churches. The current church was built in the 1750s by the Bateman family, who demolished much of the original and attached a new nave to the thirteenth-century tower. Fortunately, two Norman doorways and the elaborate chancel arch were saved and re-erected as a decorative landscape feature now known as the Shobdon Arches (left). St John the Evangelist's essentially bland exterior belies what lies within (below) – a bizarre Rococo-Gothic fantasy designed in collaboration with the Batemans' friend, Horace Walpole (of Strawberry Hill Gothick fame). It is furnished with enormous white-painted pews and an elaborate three-decker pulpit. It must have been hard for parishioners to concentrate on the droning of their priest when seated in such a distracting environment.

BELOW: Maesyronen Chapel, Glasbury-on-Wye, Radnorshire, was established in 1696 and is a perfectly preserved example of an early Nonconformist meeting house. The recently passed Act of Tolerance had paved the way for Methodism to become an accepted part of Welsh life, and gatherings no longer had to be held furtively. Chapel services developed into occasions of almost theatrical passion, with emotively delivered sermons rousing congregations to respond with passionate hymn singing: a source of sheer enjoyment which developed into a social ritual continued in the tradition of Welsh choral singing.

RIGHT: St Mary, Capel-y-fin, Brecknockshire, lies at the foot of the Gospel Pass, a narrow twisting road over the Black Mountains linking Hay-on-Wye and Abergavenny. Almost entirely enveloped by ancient yew trees, the diminutive, whitewashed church was built in 1762, replacing an earlier chapel of ease on the same site, the porch being added half a century later. The church's most endearing feature is a lopsided wooden belfry containing two bells – although, apart from the farmhouse directly opposite, it is difficult to detect whence a congregation might appear in response to their prompting.

abbeys and monasteries

Two of the main monastic orders, the Cistercians and Augustinians, are fairly evenly represented along either side of the Welsh border in the Marches. The first decades of the tenth century saw a renewed interest in monasticism, but the events of 1066 brought dramatic changes, not least the fact that most abbeys subsequently had a French abbot imposed upon them. The attendant language and cultural differences made the early post-Conquest years a difficult period for already established English monasteries. However, the majority of those in the Marches were new foundations, established by the Norman Marcher lords on land they received from the king in recognition of loyal service during the Conquest. For many such patrons, the endowment of a monastery was considered highly beneficial to their chances of getting a favourable hearing when called to the Final Judgement.

The ruins that survive throughout the region perfectly illustrate the grandeur of even the remotest establishments. It is readily apparent how complex and costly they must have been to build and sustain. It is rare to find monasteries that were not plundered for their stone after the Dissolution, but it was usually the domestic buildings rather than the churches that suffered such a fate. Arches are rounded in typical Norman fashion and the supporting pillars tend towards the large and functional.

Monastic life, always austere, was rendered even more trying in the Marches by cross-border raids by the Welsh. It must have been hard to endure the repeated loss of livestock, religious treasures and manuscripts, knowing that as soon as they had been replaced or restored the same fate could befall them again. Henry VIII is perceived as being personally responsible for monasticism's demise by bringing in the Dissolution of the Monasteries in 1536, but in reality many of the smaller houses were scarcely viable, and would have succumbed anyway through poverty and neglect.

BELOW: The Augustinian abbey of Haughmond, Shropshire, dedicated to St John the Evangelist, occupies a rocky hillside a couple of miles from the important Marcher town of Shrewsbury. Because level ground was at a premium, the normal east–west monastic layout had to be abandoned in favour of a north–south axis. The abbey's church has completely disappeared, but surviving remains include a rare double cloister, the infirmary and a lavishly appointed abbot's lodging, which was further enhanced when transformed into a grand mansion by the abbey's post-Dissolution owners.

RIGHT: Buildwas Abbey, Shropshire, was established in 1135 by Roger de Clinton, Bishop of Coventry, as a daughter house of Cumbria's Furness Abbey. The substantial remains of the Cistercian monastery sit adjacent to the River Severn, just a short distance upstream from Ironbridge, birthplace of the Industrial Revolution. Despite the abbey's being poorly endowed and never housing more than a dozen monks, the church, now roofless, possessed an impressive scale and proportion. The style is Transitional, in which pillars retained their solid form, but the heavy, rounded, Norman arches were beginning to show signs of stretching upwards into a more pointed shape. Although Buildwas experienced raids during the Welsh rebellions, it was perhaps perceived as scarcely worth much effort, and any damage to the fabric was slight.

LEFT: St Milburga's Priory, Much Wenlock, Shropshire, is a perfect example of the Cluniac ethos of glorifying God through elaborate ritual amid magnificent surroundings. It was founded in 1070 by one of William I's staunchest supporters, Roger Montgomery, who had also been a benefactor to the powerful monastic house of Cluny in Burgundy. There had been religious foundations on this site for centuries prior to the Conquest, and Montgomery sought to re-establish that tradition by inviting a group of monks over from France. As the priory flourished and grew wealthy, money was ploughed into a church rebuilding programme during the thirteenth century. The scale and grandeur of that work is apparent in a portion of the south transept, which has survived to almost full height. But the site's most visually stunning feature dates back to the earlier Norman building: the interlaced blind arcading on the chapter house is utterly captivating in its geometric perfection, a lasting tribute to the skill of stonemasons working almost a millennium ago. One wonders how twenty-first-century architecture will be perceived after a similar passage of time.

BELOW AND RIGHT:
Dore Abbey, Abbeydore, Herefordshire, was founded as a Cistercian abbey in 1147. Most of its buildings were plundered for stone after the Dissolution, but the church chancel, crossing and transepts were restored by Viscount Scudamore during the seventeenth century to serve the local community as a place of worship. Large quantities of oak were used to refurbish the interior, including around 200 tons on the roof alone. However, despite the visually warming effect of an elaborate screen and other furnishings, the cavernous space precludes any sense of intimacy, and even on a sunny summer's day the chill of antiquity prevails. Although most of the other monastic buildings have disappeared, there are the scant remains of the cloisters and chapter house to explore; the ambulatory around the chancel has been turned into something of an archaeological museum. The floor is almost completely covered with assorted fragments of masonry, elegantly carved capitals and pieces of statuary. Some exhibits have been identified and labelled, others will probably remain forever as mysterious pieces of an uncompleted jigsaw.

BELOW AND OPPOSITE: Llanthony Priory, near Abergavenny, Monmouthshire, was established in remote countryside in 1118. The Honddu valley lies on the eastern flanks of the Black Mountains, and runs parallel with Offa's Dyke and the English border. Unfortunately, the Augustinian canons soon discovered that their location, as well as being beautiful, was also extremely vulnerable. A Welsh uprising after the death of Henry I sought to drive all vestiges of the Norman Conquest from Welsh soil, and the priory was abandoned for some fifty years. It also suffered at the hands of both English and Welsh forces during Owain Glyndwr's campaign at the turn of the fifteenth century and never really recovered, limping on towards the Dissolution in a parlous state of physical and financial decline. The surviving buildings date from the late twelfth and early thirteenth centuries, and were completed in a rather austere form of Transitional architecture. An hotel has long occupied the western tower and adjacent buildings, and was once visited by the Victorian diarist, the Rev. Francis Kilvert. He bemoaned the arrival of organised tourism to such a remote spot, grumbling, 'If there is one thing more hateful than another, it is being told what to admire and having objects pointed out to one with a stick.'

winter

Winter is absolutely the best time to be striding out over
the Shropshire Hills or perhaps further south, overlooking Herefordshire's Golden Valley and the Black
Mountains beyond. On crisp, clear days when the sun
is bright, but never seems to rise far above the horizon,
the acutely angled light illuminates every detail and
texture of the landscape with startling clarity. Those who
live and work on the land in the more remote villages
will be battening down the hatches and preparing for
winter, regardless of suggestions that harsh ones are a
thing of the past. Livestock is brought down from the
higher pastures and vast piles of split logs seem to
occupy every available space around farmyard and
cottage garden alike. By the time December rolls along,
nature has already slipped into a well-rehearsed state of
suspended animation, waiting patiently for the first
snowdrops to give the all clear so that another year can
get under way.

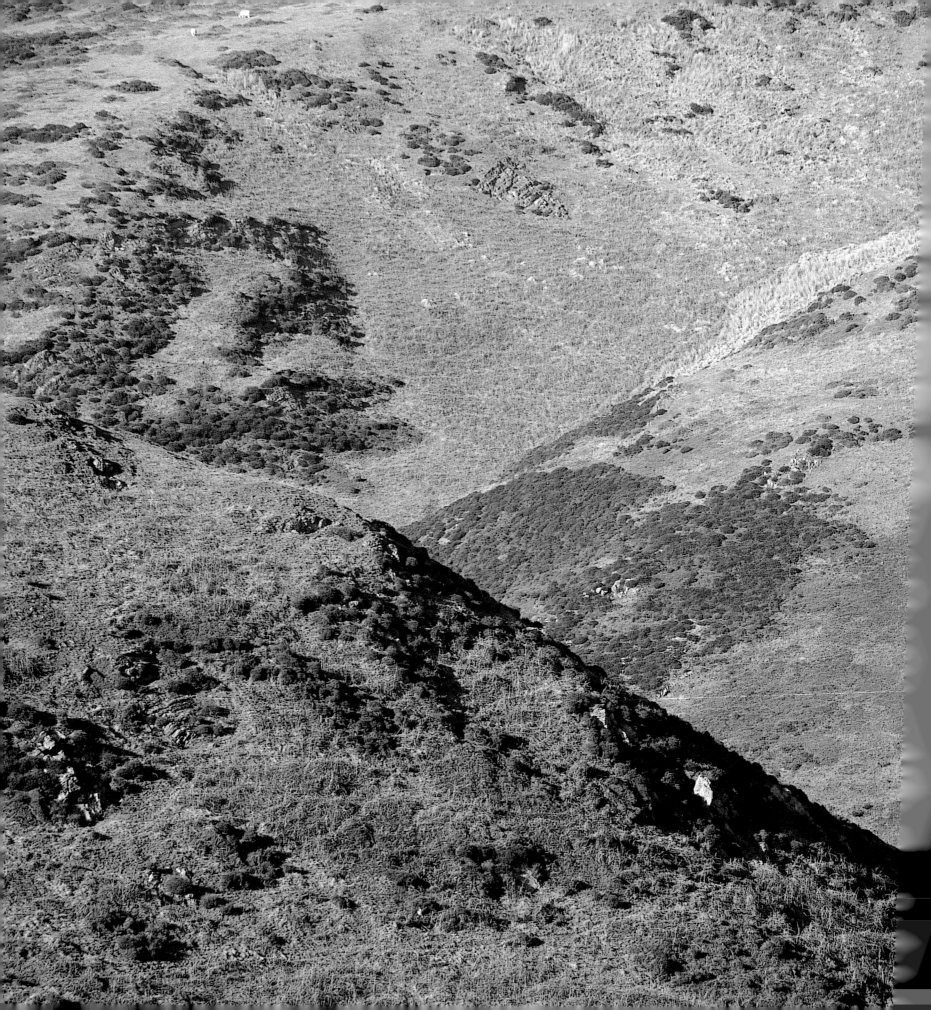

OPPOSITE: Diagonal lines created by the deep rifts of the valleys piercing the Shropshire Hills instil a strong geometric symmetry to the landscape. The composition is aided by the tones and textures of dead bracken and a sense of scale imparted by two sheep at the upper left.

RIGHT: Trees are a rare feature on the exposed upper slopes of the Long Mynd, but this twisted and stunted hawthorn makes a dramatic foreground feature. The deep ultramarine blue sky was achieved by using a polarising filter, while a wide angle lens gives the tree a more dominant role.

LEFT: Massed ranks of conifers have become an integral part of the Marches' landscape, and remain impervious to seasonal changes. When viewed from a distance en masse, they can create an unsightly dark blot on the countryside, but are quite photogenic when viewed from within a plantation.

BELOW: The golden light of a winter sunset suffuses the exterior of this half-timbered house with an artificially romantic warm glow; in reality, it is in the process of succumbing to old age and gravity.

RIGHT: The first frosts of winter coat a cluster of surviving beech leaves with a grainy, white deposit. Limiting the depth of field throws the subject into sharper relief by rendering the background out of focus.

BELOW: An overnight ground frost gives this view from the Stiperstones additional depth and colour. Looking out over the tranquil scene, it is hard to believe that this was once an area of intense lead-mining activity. Towards the latter part of the nineteenth century, this region produced over 10 per cent of the nation's lead ore requirement.

THESE PAGES: The Stiperstones ridge is a paradise for geologists, nature lovers and, above all, photographers! The Ordovician quartzite rock from which the ridge is formed was shattered during the last Ice Age to create the jagged, boulder-strewn landscape of today. The quality of light falling upon a subject is always of paramount importance in the creation of a good image, especially when photographing rock formations such as these. Winter can be especially rewarding, as the sun's low angle persists throughout the day, resulting in strong textures and clearly etched geological detail. Low sun can also be harnessed to create dramatic silhouettes, although the technique of shooting directly into it does require a bit of trial and error.

BELOW: The larch is a rarity among conifers in being deciduous, and exhibits quite startling shades of colour through the changes of season. Its delicate, frond-like leaves are particularly photogenic when covered in a layer of hoar frost.

OPPOSITE: After heavy snowfall, the conifer plantations of Radnor Forest become even more silent than normal. Snow deadens all sound, creating a disconcertingly eerie sensation. The advent of four-wheel drive vehicles has made the lives of farmers and shepherds significantly easier during the harsher winter months, but for those whose livelihood is derived from the land, this season can be one of worrying uncertainty.

OVERLEAF: The road into Wales from Hay-on-Wye skirts the northern bluff of the Black Mountains before descending towards Talgarth. From there one gets a spectacular view of the Brecon Beacons, whose highest summit, Pen y Fan (886m/ 2,900ft) is also the most distinctively shaped and recognisable throughout the whole area.

OPPOSITE: *The Welsh Marches may occasionally get a harsher than normal winter, but even around the upper slopes of the Black Mountains it is seldom cold enough to freeze fast-running streams. A succession of hard frosts can result in residual areas of icing, where water splashing on to surrounding rocks or grass becomes frozen into crystal versions of stalactites and stalagmites.*

RIGHT: Snowdrops surrounding the nineteenth-century gravestone of a local civic official and his wife herald the imminent arrival of spring and the beginning of another chapter in nature's saga.

index